WHY I
HATE
TEXAS

An Insider's Guide to Everything Wrong with the Lone Star State

By Michelle M. Haas

ISBN 978-1-941324-93-6

Introduction

I've spent most of my adult life reading and writing about Texas history and culture. I've written a few books about it, and have published dozens more, but have never endeavored to write a book about why I love Texas. To me, the wonders of Texas are ineffable, and, frankly, more capable writers have already "effed" the topic pretty well. I decided to approach this animal from the other end, and instead compose a book about what I despise about the land of my nativity. I figured it would get the point across just the same.

To the reader so anxious to own an anti-Texas book that he didn't read its description before buying—yes, I'm talking to you—now foaming at the mouth, frantically pecking out a one-star review because the book lacks the hate he so desperately craved...gotcha!

To my fellow Texans who understand the need for a book like this one, I lovingly dedicate it to you.

God & Texas,

Michelle M. Haas
Furman Plaza
Corpus Christi TX

Why I Hate Texas:

8

10

11

12

14

.

16

18

20

22

24

26

28

30

32

34

36

38

40

42

43

44

46

47

48

50

52

54

56

58

60

62

64

66

68

70

72

74

76

78

80

82

84

86

88

90

92

94

95

96

98

100

Why I Hate Texas:

102

103

104

106

107

108

109

110

112

114

116

118

120

121

122

124

126

128

129

130

131

132

134

136

138

140

142

144

146

147

148

149

150

151

152

153

154

156

158

160

162

164

166

167

168

169

170

172

174

176

177

178

179

180

181

182

184

186

188

189

190

192

194

195

196

198

200

201

202

204

205

206

207

208

209

210

211

212

214

216

217

218

220

222

223

224

225

226

228

229

230

232

234

236

238

239

240

241

242

244

246

247

248

250